Spotlight on Spelling

by Hugh O'Connell

Introduction

The spelling strategies in this booklet can be applied to primary and secondary school pupils. The strategies are selected from 'good practice' which has proved to be effective for developing spelling across the age range. It is important to emphasize that the booklet is concerned with ***practical*** strategies for teachers to consider for supporting pupils in learning how to spell in the context of National Curriculum subject areas.

Organisation of the booklet

The booklet is divided into the following sections:

The Literacy Hour

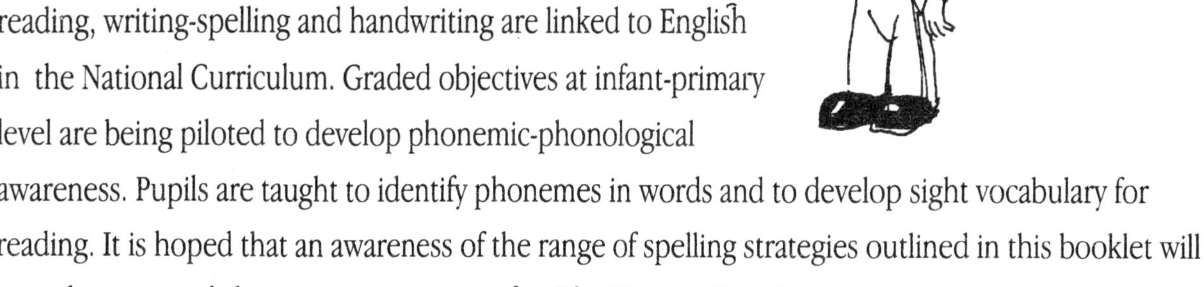

The National Literacy Project involves 'The Literacy Hour' devised to help raise standards of literacy in primary schools. Teaching objectives to develop reading, writing-spelling and handwriting are linked to English in the National Curriculum. Graded objectives at infant-primary level are being piloted to develop phonemic-phonological awareness. Pupils are taught to identify phonemes in words and to develop sight vocabulary for reading. It is hoped that an awareness of the range of spelling strategies outlined in this booklet will contribute towards language programmes for 'The Literacy Hour'.

What is a 'spelling strategy'?

It is a specific and reliable method for learning to spell, using sensory channels to memorise a blend, word or words for accurate retrieval.

Characteristics of effective Spelling Strategies:

 Spelling develops when the 'memory departments' begin to identify and retain the sequential look, shape, sound and 'feel' of a word.

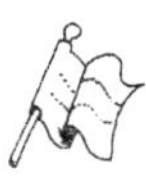 An effective approach is to draw upon either all or selected sensory channels: visual, auditory, oral, tactile, motor-kinaesthetic.

 Spelling is linked to a cursive style of handwriting whereupon the 'grapho-pattern' of a word is felt by movements of the hand—in fact, spelling and handwriting should be perceived as 'twins'.

 Learning how to spell can be achieved using different strategies for different kinds of learners.

 Spelling becomes more meaningful when linked to writing—in fact spelling supports writing.

 Regular revision is essential to develop spelling skills.

 Through analysis of language, spelling develops thinking skills.

Identifying Pupils with Spelling Difficulties

The application of a new spelling strategy should be considered if any of the following signs **regularly** occur:

 frequent misspellings or 'miscues' involving 'high frequency' keywords (for a list of the high-frequency words—see page 17)

 the regular use by a pupil of a particular strategy is not proving effective

 a poor attitude or a low self-esteem of the pupil towards spelling

 an increasing reluctance to write

 an avoidance of spelling revision by the pupil

 behaviour difficulties arising in spelling or writing activities

However, for a pupil with a severe spelling difficulty, such as arising from dyslexia, a detailed assessment will be required to identify appropriate spelling strategies, which can be applied by a trained specialist teacher providing individual support.

Spelling Strategies and Individual Education Plans

Pupils placed on a Stage 2, 3, 4, 5 of the Code of Practice requiring support for identified spelling difficulties should have the spelling strategy which has been selected to help them indicated on their Individual Education Plan. Any subsequent review of the I.E.P. will provide an appropriate time for assessing whether the selected spelling strategies are proving effective.

Basic Checklist before selecting a Spelling Strategy

A useful resource that includes the relevant checklists is
The Basic Skills Record of Achievement (Desktop Publications 1997)
For a pupil with spelling problems it is important to check the following:

a) *Basic phonic skills*

 recognises the names of all letters in the alphabet

 can correctly recall sounds of all letters in the alphabet

b) *Handwriting skills:*

 can correctly form initial letters of the alphabet

 is beginning to develop a cursive writing style—for example, can write name in

joined-up writing

c) *Memorv skills*

 from observation can memorise and recall pictures in sequence

 from observation can memorise and recall symbols and letters in sequence

It is particularly useful to read Tony Buzan (1991) for further approaches to develop memory training. This has implications not only for developing spelling skills but is useful for work in other National Curriculum subject areas!

d) *Pupil attitude*

The interpersonal relationship between the pupil and the teacher should develop from achieving success in spelling. However, the teacher will need to exercise professional expertise to restore a positive attitude towards spelling in a pupil who has low self-esteem as a speller. This is an extremely important and delicate task, which should be delivered through graded and achievable spelling steps appropriate for the pupil.

It is important to emphasize that these strategies are not definitive, nor placed in ascending order of effectiveness. Although it may appear that some strategies overlap, it is how and when they are used which will demonstrate their effectiveness. Furthermore, some strategies may work for some pupils and not others, because we all have different ways of learning to memorise. What is important is that teachers are aware of the range of spelling strategies available. The suitability of a spelling strategy can be checked by closely observing a pupil's style of learning and writing. A spelling strategy is only effective if it works. If it's not producing progress, change it.

List of Spelling Strategies

1. Memory Training
2. Oral-Tactile
3. Oral - Motor/Kinaesthetic
4. Phonological—rhyming patterns
5. Phonic
6. Multisensory
7. Look/Remember-Cover-Write-Check
8. Look-Say-Cover-Say-Write-Check
9. SOS—Simultaneous Oral Spelling
10. Syllabification
11. Words within words
12. Visual and Sound Families
13. Extending Strings using Affixes
14. Selected Spelling Rules
15. Discovering the Rule
16. Serial Probability—Generalization
17. Word origins/meanings
18. Morphemes
19. Mnemonics
20. Dictionaries
21. Personal Word Books
22. IT\Spellcheckers
23. Visual prompt—Highlighting
24. Spelling partners
25. Spelling games/activities
26. Deliberately difficult words
27. Handwriting
28. Dictation
29. Reading
30. Pupil's Personal Interests
31. Pupil's Experiences
32. Pupil's Preferred Specialist Subject
33. Life and Social Skills

Outline of Spelling Strategies

I. Memory Training

This should be considered a prerequisite strategy for learning to
spell—progressing from pictures and sounds to symbols. Ensure that
the memory task matches the capability and level of the learner, whether
an infant or teenager.

1. Memorise one, two, three progressing to seven, *objects* or *pictures*
2. Memorise one two, three progressing to seven, *sounds*
3. Memorise one, two, three progressing to seven, *symbols*
4. Memorise and write one, two, three, progressing to seven, *letters*

2. Oral-Tactile ('finger' spelling) materials—sand tray, felt, plastic letters

1. Look at and say the letter/word
2. Say letter/word as you write letter/word with finger on 'touch-sensitive' material (e.g. sand, sandpaper, felt) to help 'feel' the shape of letter/word
3. Cover the letter/word
4. Write and say the letter/word in joined-up writing in sand, on felt, or by 'skywriting'
5. Check the letter/word

3. Oral—Motor/Kinaesthetic

1. Look at and say the letter/word (written in large-sized letters)
2. Trace over the letter/word with crayon/pen/pencil
3. Cover the letter/word
4. Say and Write the letter/word in joined-up writing on paper
5. Check the letter/word

4. Phonological—rhyming patterns

Spelling by analogy by identifying common rhyming and spelling patterns in a group of words.

1. Example words: *bake*   *lake*   *make*   *take*
2. Identify the common rhyming pattern—*ake*
3. Specify the number of words to build with the common rhyming/spelling pattern
4. Write sentence(s) to include as many of the words identified
5. Build words using 'analogy of similar phoneme patterns but different spellings'—
   cried fried guide hide lied   pride ride side tide tried

5.   Phonic

Sound-symbol correspondence. For example, one syllable/cvc words. Identify the individual sound and match with the written symbol

1.   Look at word   *bat*
2.   Say clearly individual regular sounds: *b - a - t*
3.   Cover the word
4.   Write the word saying individual letter sounds
5.   Check the word

6.   Multisensory—simultaneous inclusive application of all sensory channels

1.   Look—say the whole word clearly—listen to the sound/syllables
2.   Look—listen as you name the letters in the word (If the target word is already written in large letters use a finger to trace/touch and feel the shape of letters/word)
3.   Cover the word
4.   Say the word and write it in joined-up writing
5.   Check the word

7.   Look\Remember - Cover - Write - Check

1.   Look closely at the word: *right*
     It is also useful to link it with a common pattern: *fight, night, right*
     Close eyes—try to remember the word - if necessary, look again
2.   Cover the word
3.   Write the word in joined-up writing
4.   Check the word

8.   Look - Say - Cover - Say/Write - Check

1.   Look closely at the word: *right*
2.   Say the word: *right*
3.   Name the letters: *'r - i - g - h - t'*
4.   Cover the word
5.   Say the word as you write in joined-up writing
6.   Check the word

9.   SOS—Simultaneous Oral Spelling

1.   Say the whole word—articulate clearly
2.   Name and write the word, naming the letters as the word is written
3.   Say the word
4.   Check the word is written correctly
5.   Repeat 'look-write' naming each letter—check twice
6.   Practise same procedure for six consecutive days

10. Syllabification

1. Look and clearly say word: *enjoyment*
2. Break into syllables and say: *en - joy - ment*
3. Say clearly while tapping out the syllables
4. Repeat at least three times
5. Write out the word in joined up writing saying the syllables
6. Check the word

11. Words within words

1. Look at the word: *computer*
2. Try to find words within the word: *com**put**er*
3. Say the whole word
4. Say the word stressing the identified word within the bigger word
5. Cover the word
6. Say and write the word in joined up writing
7. Check the word

12. Visual and Sound Families

Find words with similar patterns:

1   Look at the word: *strange*

2   Break it into families and link it with words containing similar patterns

str -   **str**ap

strong

street

stream

strap

ange-   gr**ange**

r**anger**

st**ranger**

st**rangest**

st**rangely**

3   Say the words stressing the highlighted parts
4   Create a sentence using the target word
5   Cover the target word
6   Write the word stressing the highlighted parts
7   Check the word

13. Extending Strings using Affixes (prefixes and suffixes)

1. Look at the word: *friend*

2. Attach affixes to the word: *friend**ly***

        ***un**friendly*

        *friend**liest***

        *friend**ship***

        *friend**less***

        be**friend**ed

3. Create a sentence using the target word

4. Cover the target word

5. Say/write the target word

6. Check the word

14. Selected Spelling Rules

Too many rules can prove confusing, but this selection provide an idea of what is available:

1. For *e* sound

   i before *e* except after *c* :   *bel**ie**ve; rel**ie**f - rec**ei**ve*

2. For *a* or *i* sound

   e before *i* :   *a* sound - ***ei**ght, w**ei**ght, v**ei**n*

           i sound - h**ei**ght, **ei**ther, n**ei**ther

3. Plurals of nouns ending in *f* or *fe*:

   usually just add *s*:   *safe - safe**s**,   roof - roof**s***

   sometimes change *f* to *v* and add *es:*   *calf - cal**ves**; wife - wi**ves**; wolf - wol**ves***

4. Add *ies* to singular nouns ending in *y:*

       *lady - lad**ies**;   enemy - enem**ies**;   try - tr**ies**;*

5. Add *s* to singular nouns ending with a vowel and *y*:

       *journey - journey**s**;   chimney - chimney**s**;   valley - valley**s**;*

6. Add *es* to singular nouns ending in *ch, x, s, sh*:

       *witch**es**,   box**es**   address**es**   crash**es***

7. Add *ing* to verbs - unless the verb ends with *e* as the final consonant then drop *e* and add *ing*:

       *come - com**ing** ; exercise - exercis**ing** ; breathe - breath**ing***

8. For words of more than one syllable that end in a single vowel and a *single l*, double the *l*:

       *travel - trave**ll**ing;   level - leve**ll**ing;   tunnel - tunne**ll**ing*

9. For words of more than one syllable with stress on the final syllable that end in a single vowel followed by a single consonant, double the final letter:

       *be**gin** - be**ginn**ing;   prefer - prefe**rr**ing;   forget - forge**tt**ing*

15. Discovering the Spelling Rule

A useful strategy for learning spelling rules is to provide related words and ask pupils whether they can 'discover the rule' which can be applied to the words! This process of 'self-discovery' may be meaningful and helpful for some pupils.

Further strategies:

- display rules with examples on a wall display, using colour to highlight appropriate changes in a word when the rule is applied
- target one rule for a specific period, e.g. a week or month
- 'share rules' by having a group explain the rule to another group
- insert rule in individual spelling books
- select one rule for homework revision
- teach/revise rules as a regular part of class spelling activities.

16. Serial Probability—Generalizing

Identifying from a group of words spelling *probabilities,* which can be applied to spell other words containing similar sounds:

Word Group:

bright	*bite*	*fight*	*fright*	*light*	*might*
night	*quite*	*right*	*sight*	*tight*	*white*

Subgroups selected:

a) **bright** **fight** **fright** **light** **might** **night** **right** **sight** **tight**

b) **bite** **quite** **white**

Generalization: the final syllable of a word containing long *i* followed by a *t* sound is probably spelt:

i-g-h-t or **i-t-e**

17. Word origins/meanings

This strategy explores the origin of English words and can be a most insightful and rewarding study in its own right. It also explores and demonstrates the assimilated richness of the language.

Olde English:		initial consonant (*wh*); vowel digraph (*aw, ew, ow*)
Latin:		ject (throw): *deject, project, reject*
Greek:		pathos (feeling): *apathy, empathy, sympathy*
Old Norse /Viking:		taka (take): *mistake, overtake, undertaker*
French:		que: *queue, unique, grotesque*

Italy:	*balcony*	Spanish:	*armadillo*
Dutch:	*yacht*	Arabic:	*harem, mufti*
Eskimo	*anorak*	Gujurati:	*bungalow*

18. Morphemes

A morpheme is a meaning or grammatical function that cannot be further subdivided. Studying the same morpheme in a variety of words provides an effective teaching tool for focusing attention on how words are put together.

Morpheme Building:

1. Look and say the keyword clearly - *happiness*
2. Divide keyword into morphemes - *hap -pi -ness*
3. Clearly say the morphemes
4. Extract the morpheme for word building: **hap**
5. Build new words using the selected morpheme

	hap	*py*
	hap	*pen*
mis	**hap**	
s	**hap**	*en*
	hap	*hazard*
s	**hap**	*e*

6. Discuss the meaning of the words
7. Select the target word(s)
8. Look and clearly say target word(s)
9. Cover word(s)
10. Say and write word(s)
11. Check word(s)

19. Mnemonics

Create a verse, rhyme or sentence to spell the blend\word

For example:

O and U come together

When its stormy weather,

For they will help build a house

In which can live a little mouse!

*Silent **e** may take some time to decide to like me.*

***Because—b**ig elephants **c**an **a**lways **u**nderstand **s**mall **e**lephants*

***necess**ary—one collar and two sleeves*

***accommo**dation—Colin and Carol **m**ay **m**arry*

20. Dictionaries

1. Pupil should know the alphabet sequence
2. Use the mnemonic **E**arly **M**orning **S**unshine—**EMS** to introduce important markers:

    A ----------E-----------M-------------S------------Z

3. Pupils should look for words written by teachers
4. Use dictionaries to explore the roots/meanings of words
5. Use dictionaries to revise words
6. Use the ACE dictionary (LDA, Ely, Cambridge) to develop auditory training to identify short and long vowels

21. Personal dictionary-word book

1. Write the spelling strategy on the first page with examples of how to apply the strategy
2. Enter new words/topic keywords in alphabetic sequence
3. Use this to help spell high-frequency words/topic keywords
4. Create a sentence to include target word(s)
5. Use this to help with revision of words

22. IT programmes/Spellcheckers

1. Most word processing programmes these days possess inbuilt spell checking facilities
2. There are also many useful 'drill and practice' programmes for developing spelling such as: Starspell Plus (Fisher Marriott); Hi-Spell (Xavier); Superspell (4Mation); Spell It 3 (Davidson)
3. Spellcheckers such as the Franklin Spellmaster allow pupils to check their own spellings
4. Redrafting of writing on computers emphasizes the proper purpose of spelling—to help communicate through writing
5. Most recent IT developments allow direct transcription from voice input into written form
6. Spelling is inbuilt within the drafting process

23. Visual Prompts—Highlighting

1. Display particular keywords/blends by using colours to highlight them
2. Display the words most frequently misspelt in pupils' writing
3. Ask the pupils to display words they find in their own writing
4. Update visual prompts, e.g. *Keyword\Blend of the Week*

24. Spelling Partners

1. A partner can observe/check any spelling strategies applied by the other partner
2. Partners can 'test' each other
3. The use of partners should also be considered for revising spellings

25. Spelling Games and Activities

1. These (whether its 'I Spy'; 'Spellmaster'; 'Hangman'; 'Shannon's Game' [First Steps]; 'Spelling Investigations' [National Literacy Project]) are an important part of any spelling programme

2. Spelling games are also available as I.T. software. For example, 'Spell It 3' [Davidson]; Superspell [4Mation]

3. It is important to ensure that all spelling sessions should contain some games—to reinforce or revise in a fun way

26. Deliberately Difficult Words!

1. This approach can be used with partners, small groups or a whole class.

2. The purpose is to make pupils think about spelling from sounds, by generalizing etc.

3. Deliberately difficult words can also be used to develop dictionary skills/use of ACE dictionary

4. Correct spellings can be presented through phonemes, letters, syllables

5. This strategy should also be considered for challenging more able spellers

27. Handwriting

1. Ensure individual letters are correctly formed

2. Encourage pupils to begin cursive\joined-up writing

3. Use handwriting practice to learn new blends\letter patterns

28. Dictation

1. Dictation should be used to check any spelling which has been previously taught

2. It is a very useful strategy for revising a range of spellings: specific blends; topic keywords; high-frequency words

3. The amount of dictation (a sentence/ a few lines / a longer paragraph) will depend on the spelling ability of the pupils

29. Reading

1. When reading together—make sure the child articulates the words clearly

2. Name the letters in selected high-frequency words

3. Look for words with similar letter patterns/sounds

4. Early Years—build simple rhymes using a selected context word:

   e.g.   context word: ***ran***

   The man ran after the van.

5. Primary/Secondary—reading through decoding by:
   syllabification; segmenting words; origin, meaning of words; developing dictionary skills

Strategies 30, 31, 32, 33 should be considered for pupils who are 'reluctant spellers'. These strategies can also be combined as 'a personal approach to spelling' which is adapted to suit a pupil's interests, experiences, needs etc.

30. Pupil's Personal Interests

The pupil states their interest, for example, football, pop music, fashion, fishing, etc.

1.   Make a short list of keywords (3–6) related to the pupil's interest

2.   Look at the spelling of a keyword, for example, *Manchester United*

3.   (Possible strategy: Words within words)

      Look for words within the keyword: **Man-chest-er**

4.   Build words from letter patterns identified in the keyword:

      Manchester   **best, rest, test, west**

5.   The pupil creates sentences using the keywords identified

31. Pupil's Experiences

This should follow the same approach as strategy 30, working from the pupil's personal experience, for example, a holiday, a shopping trip, work experience, a day out with the family etc.

1.   Keywords can be identified from pupil's comments

2.   Choose an appropriate strategy to use with the spelling of these keywords

3.   Revision—Get the pupil to talk about his/her experiences again and check if the pupil can still spell the keywords

32. Pupil's Preferred Specialist Subject

This approach uses the pupil's interest in a single subject or topic area. Any curriculum subject/topic area can be considered. Select keywords related to the subject/topic and apply an appropriate strategy for learning to spell the words.

33. Life and Social Skills

This is spelling for 'living and working in the community'. Strategies and keywords should be selected as a result of discussion with students.

1.   Look at spellings required for filling in forms

2.   Look at spellings required for filling in job applications

3.   Note words used in adverts, magazines, road signs, etc. and build up a 'social sight' vocabulary

      For example: *men, women, entrance, exit*

                        Admission, No Entry, Danger

4.   Create sentences to include target words

5.   Revision: Check spellings as they arise in discussion

All state schools follow programmes of study in National Curriculum subject areas. This has important implications from the viewpoint of teaching spelling, as there tends to be inadequate time for direct class teaching of spelling. It must also be recognised that spelling and writing expand in volume and frequency as pupils progress through the key stages of the National Curriculum. Therefore, the criteria for teaching spelling must consider:

- subject specialist vocabulary that needs to be understood by pupils for application in writing
- the spellings required for the 'writing subjects'—English, Science, Geography, History, Modern Languages, Religious Education
- that conceptual demands in the use of subject vocabulary increase with corresponding frequency in writing, as pupils move from primary through to secondary school and toward examination courses

Examples of spelling strategies to be included in Individual Education Plans for primary and secondary pupils at Key Stages 1, 2, 3, 4, are included on pages 16 to 23, in order to illustrate how primary and secondary schools can use a range of spelling strategies linked to the learning of high-frequency keywords/subject-specific vocabulary.

Subject	Key Stage		Keywords
English	Reception	Key Stage 1	Sight recognition words
English	Primary	Key Stage 2	High-frequency keywords
History	Primary	Key Stage 2	History keywords
Eng. Lit - Drama	Secondary	Key Stage 3	Literature/Drama keywords
Biology	Secondary	Key Stage 4	Biology Keywords

a	day	it	she
all	do	like	the
am	for	look	they
and	get	me	this
are	go	mum	to
at	going	my	up
away	he	no	was
big	help	of	we
can	here	on	went
cat	I	play	yes
come	in	said	you
dad	is	see	

(Adapted into alphabetic order from Sight Recognition Words—National Literacy Project, 1997)

Planning for Spelling and S.E.N. in the Literacy Hour

The reading of sight recognition words will be a key objective in the Literacy Hour—National Literacy Project. The spelling of the keywords can be linked to the writing (word-sentence) section of the Literacy Hour.

Individual Education Plans

Reception children with special educational needs are likely to have I.E.P.'s containing literacy targets. Where appropriate, early basic spelling skills will be included in these targets.

Example I.E.P.

Background information

Jamie attended a playgroup and received speech therapy within a small group. Jamie has 'temper tantrums' and is placed at Stage 2 on the S.E.N. register. He can recognise two letters of the alphabet ('a' and 'j') and traces over words written by his teacher. The noun selected as a target *('cat')* was linked to direct experience—Jamie owns a cat.

Spelling Target: To recognise three letters of the alphabet in order to build two sight recognition words to make a simple sentence *(The cat).*

Letters selected:	From sight recognition words *(the cat):* a c e h t
Spelling Strategies:	Visual / oral / tactile / phonological approach
Materials:	Sand tray, plastic letters
Revision:	Daily revision for four sessions (5 minutes)
	Tracing over the two-word sentence *(The cat)*
	Drawings of cats with the printed model two-word sentence.

a	about	after	all	am	an
and	are	as	at	back	be
because	bed	big	but	called	came
can	come	could	dad	day	did
do	door	down	for	found	get
go	going	good	got	had	has
have	he	her	him	his	home
house	I	if	in	into	is
it	like	little	man	me	mum
my	next	no	not	of	off
on	once	one	our	out	over
people	play	put	ran	said	saw
school	see	she	so	some	that
the	their	then	them	there	they
time	to	took			
two	up	very			
was	we	went			
were	what	when			
will	with	would			
you					

(From 'The Hot Top' [DTP]. Adapted from 'Word for Word'—Dee Reid [1989] LDA, Cambridge)

Example I.E.P.

Background Information

Katy is a Y3 pupil of low ability with reading and spelling difficulties. She is placed on Stage 2 of the S.E.N. Register. A review of the I.E.P. by the S.E.N. Co-ordinator revealed that Katy was three years behind in spelling, as measured on a norm-referenced spelling test. Analysis of Katy's free writing showed she had difficulty in spelling the following high-frequency words:

  going have our said their would

The SEN Co-ordinator discussed the results with Katy's class teacher, and the following short term spelling target was agreed for Katy's I.E.P.:

Learning Target: To spell six high-frequency words identified from free writing

Keywords selected: *going have our said their would*

Before learning the selected words the following areas were checked:

* recognition of letter names/sounds:

    vowels   a, e, i, o, u

    consonants d g h l n r s t v w

* handwriting: a check of all the letters in the identified words

Two spelling strategies were selected:

1. Look/Say - Cover - Write/Say - Check *(all target words)*
2. Words within words   ***(going, said, their)***

Reinforcement: Writing activity: create sentences to include the target words

    Write the words in Personal Wordbook

Revision: Fortnightly spelling practice on computer using 'drill and practice' software

    with further high-frequency words

    Revise at home with parent (arranged at I.E.P. review)

The Spanish Armada

ago	Armada	army	battle	blockade
cannon	Catholics	century	Drake	events
famous	Elizabethan	England	galleon	heroes
invasion	maps	maritime	national	navy
period	Protestant	queen	raids	sailor
ships	soldiers	Spain	Tudor	voyage
war				

(From 'Keywords in Specialist Subjects' Desktop Publications 1995)

Example I.E.P.

Background information

Peter is a Y5 pupil with spelling difficulties. He is placed on Stage 2 of the S.E.N. Register. He is two years behind in spelling as measured on a norm-referenced spelling test. He likes history writing but sometimes has difficulty learning to spell new topic keywords. Current class topic is 'The Spanish Armada'.

Keywords selected:

Armada   blockade   cannon   Catholics   Elizabethan   galleon   invasion   Protestant

Selected spelling strategies: look-cover-write-check   linguistic/meaning   syllabification

words within words   spelling partner

Each word was analysed using three strategies:

For example: .   **Armada**

Word origin/meaning: *Fleet of warships sent by Spain against England in 1588*

Syllables: **Ar - ma - da**

words within words: **Arm** - *ada*

Peter was matched with a spelling partner to analyse the other five words using the same spelling strategies.

Using 'look-cover-write-check' keywords were entered at the back of Peter's History book to be checked on a weekly basis

Revision: History keywords provided part of weekly spelling homework

accent	backstage	chorus (al)	denouement
act (ion)	balcony	climax	dialogue
actor	bathos	comedian	director (ion)
actress	blaspheme	comedienne	dramatic (irony)
adaptation	brother	comedy	Elizabethan
amuse	cast	costume	emotion(al, ally, ive)
anticlimax	censor (ize)	couplet	entertain
appear (ance)	chant	courtier	entrance
applause	character	critic (al, ism, ize)	epic
aside	characterization	dance	epilogue
		daughter	exit

One example of how to use the Keywords Checklist

The *Keywords Checklist (page 21)* provides a clear structure for learning and revising the reading and spelling of subject keywords. Although this example is for Drama, it can be used with any subject.

1. Display the full list of keywords on a poster or board. Colour code them with a highlighter pen as they are selected each week for learning (e.g. week 1—blue, week 2—green, week 3—red).

2. Select six keywords from the alphabetic list to be learned in the first week.

   For example: *actor   backstage   character   comedy   dance   entertain*

3. Discuss with the pupils the spelling strategies to be adopted.

   For example: Simultaneous oral spelling;   Words within words;

   Word origin/meaning;   Syllabification

4. The pupils should write the strategies in the space provided on the checklist.

5. The pupils should write in the words for the first week in the first six spaces on the list.

6. They should refer to their checklist as they work through the strategies using a notebook.

7. For the second week, they should add six new words to their checklist, and so on, until after four weeks their checklist should be complete. Enter the date in the box provided on completion.

8. Revise the completed checklist and enter the date in the box provided.

Keywords Checklist

Subject: _______________________ Pupil: _______________________

Topic: _______________________ Year: _______________________

Strategies:

Keywords:

1. _______________________ 2. _______________________ 3. _______________________

4. _______________________ 5. _______________________ 6. _______________________

7. _______________________ 8. _______________________ 9. _______________________

10. _______________________ 11. _______________________ 12. _______________________

13. _______________________ 14. _______________________ 15. _______________________

16. _______________________ 17. _______________________ 18. _______________________

19. _______________________ 20. _______________________ 21. _______________________

22. _______________________ 23. _______________________ 24. _______________________

Date achieved: _______________________

Date revised: _______________________

Permission to photocopy

acid (+ ic)	carbohydrate	ecosystem
alga/algae	carbon	embryo
alkali (+ ne)	carbon dioxide	energy
amino acid	carnivore (drop e + ous)	environment
amoeba	characteristic	enzyme
amphibian	chlorinate (drop e + ion)	evolution
apparatus	chlorophyll	excretion
arachnid	chromosome	experiment
artery	crustacean	extinct
atmosphere		
atrium/atria	digest	fertile (drop e + ity + isation)
	dormant (drop t + cy)	fungus/fungi
bacterium/bacteria		

Grouping of specialist keywords in alphabetic order (A to F)

From 'Subject Spellchecks - Spelling for Exams' by E.G. Stirling (1992)

Note: Further keywords can be added according to the programme of study

The extent and level of subject-specific vocabulary, as illustrated in the Biology keyword list, clearly demonstrates the very formidable task confronting G.C.S.E. pupils with spelling difficulties.

The approach to applying spelling strategies for pupils at K.S. 4 should be through a process of spelling analysis and discussion between teacher and student.

Example:

Background information

William is a statemented pupil who has received individual teaching support for specific learning difficulties. Providing William attains the appropriate GCSE grades, he hopes to attend sixth form college to study mathematics, biology and media studies. He does not like using a spellchecker (too time consuming!) but does use the spell-check on his lap-top computer. In response to project work, William prioritises writing before spelling and selects the minimum of keywords to spell.

Various spelling strategies applied:

1. William applies spelling rules, syllabification and occasionally, mnemonics, to help spell the keywords.

2. His support teacher also refers to root meaning of words

    e.g. ***amphibian*** - Greek.   ***amphi:***   both—land and water

                          bios: life

In order to reinforce the meaning, the teacher suggests another word with a variation on the root meaning of *amphi*. The teacher refers to *amphitheatre* (William is very interested in drama).

    e.g. ***amphitheatre*** - Greek.   ***amphi***: both—round, oval and circular

The teacher finds that connecting words to William's personal/direct experiences is particularly helpful for William and is, therefore, another strategy for helping him to memorise important subject keywords.

Whether at primary or secondary level, linking keywords to personal interests and/or direct experiences can make the spelling process more meaningful to pupils.

(Note: William now attends sixth form college)

Although a spelling strategy can be applied and demonstrated to have been effective over a short period, it can happen that when targeted words/blends are assessed after a longer period of time, the spelling results can prove to be disappointing. Pupils appear to have forgotten what was so effectively learnt. As a result, the core keywords have to be reintroduced in addition to new words.

One reason pupils forget how to spell words is that they do not revise spelling on a regular basis. Indeed, it has been demonstrated that 'eighty percent' of what we learn is forgotten within two days! Therefore, it is **absolutely crucial** that revision should be an integral part of any spelling programme. This will enable what is held in the short term memory to be transferred to the long term memory. Otherwise, the considerable efforts applied by both teachers and pupils will be wasted.

Strategies for organising revision of spelling

This can be approached on two fronts, school-based and home-based:

1. *School based*

- *Pupils should understand the meaning of targeted words;* use them through oral activities (group discussions); apply them in writing activities and revise them on a regular basis.
- *Visual prompts,* including target words in chart form, should be displayed as a daily visual reminder for pupils.
- *High frequency keywords* could be printed on equipment/materials. They could also be displayed on the walls in specialist areas and subject workrooms.
- *Pupils should be encouraged to use a personal dictionary to self-check spelling* rather than be told how to spell keywords already written in their personal word books.
- *Revision can be integrated into the weekly class spelling routines* by specifying certain target percentages of words already learned.

- *Individual revision* of 5 to 10 minutes can be set aside daily for a pupil to self-check target words.

- *Spelling partners* are a very effective strategy for applying spelling strategies and checking spelling

- *By using IT/computers* pupils can practice words for revision on spelling programme(s)

- *Specify on Individual Education Plans* the spelling strategy and target words for revision. This provides a clear demonstration that spelling revision is valued and will be reviewed on a date specified on the I.E.P.

- *Reward tactics* can be useful. For example, as pupils go to break, lunch or leave for home ask them to spell one or two words (if right - first out!)

- *Support from senior pupils* has proved helpful for developing reading and should be considered for spelling

- *Note:*
  Spelling revision should not be considered a chore. It is about prompting pupils so that the long-term memory can store important words that will always be needed in subjects areas.

2.   *Home Based:*

This will depend on individual circumstances and needs to be negotiated within the context of the individual education plan. Although spelling revision is firstly the responsibility of the pupil, further support can be provided by the parents. The I.E.P. can provide the mechanism for focusing on learning targets for spelling and outlining strategies which can be supported at home.

Among approaches to consider:

- Ensure the pupil understands the need for home revision and that its purpose is to reinforce as well as retain any spelling success already achieved.

- Explain to parents the spelling strategy selected for their child. This ensures that parents understand how and what their child is trying to learn.

- At the review of the I.E.P., times can be agreed for the pupil to revise spelling at home. This should be a regular weekly time, and target words should be written and dated in a revision book.

- Keep home revision very basic and clearly targeted. Do not present too many words for revision, and make sure the number fits the time slot allocated. Check with pupil after a few days. This demonstrates you value what is being done at home.

- A reward system from the home for completing spelling revision can be introduced, but this needs to be carefully considered—not forgetting that the most valued reward for a learner should be the sense of achievement and pleasure in meeting a learning challenge.

Starting up spelling revision

It needs to be emphasized that for pupils with spelling problems, organisation for revision of spelling must occur at school and at home, and needs to be on a weekly basis. Use the I.E.P. to start, monitor and reinforce spelling revision. It will be worth it!

Allan, B.V.(1989)	***Logical Spelling*** Clear presentation of spelling rules and exercises.	Collins Glasgow and London
Brand, Violet(1988)	***Spelling Made Easy*** Structured and graded materials using multisensory methods and dictation to develop spelling skills. Primary/secondary.	Egon Publishers Baldock, Herts
Bryant, P and Bradley, L. (1985)	***Children's Reading Problems*** Includes key references to the importance of rhyme and multisensory methods to develop spelling. Primary.	Blackwell, Oxford
Buzan, Tony (1991)	***Use Your Memory*** Range of techniques and systems for improving memory skills.	BBC Publications
Cripps, Charles (1988)	***A Hand for Spelling*** Series of workbooks for developing spelling focusing on letter patterns and cursive handwriting. Primary.	LDA, Ely, Cambs.
Hackman, Sue and Trickett, Liz (1996)	***Spelling 9 - 13*** Outlines spelling strategies/rules with a wide range of group activities. Upper primary/lower secondary.	Hodder Stoughton London
Huxford, Laura (1994)	***The Spelling Book*** Explains how children learn to spell. Contains simple diagnostic assessments. A graded, coherent spelling programme. Ideas for spelling activities and games.	Stanley Thornes Cheltenham
Moseley, David (1996) Moseley, David and Singleton, Gwyn (1991)	***ACE Dictionary*** ***ACE Spelling Activities*** 75 worksheets. Primary/secondary.	LDA Ely, Cambridge
Montgomery, Diane (1997)	***Developmental Spelling*** Structured series of 100 lessons using multisensory methods with phonics, linguistics. Primary/secondary.	Learning Difficulties Research Project Maldon, Essex

O'Connell, Hugh (1994) — ***The Hot Top*** — Desktop Publications Scunthorpe
Approaches for teaching the high-frequency writing words using a range of spelling strategies. Primary.

O'Connell, Hugh (1994) — ***Keywords in Specialist Subjects*** — Desktop Publications Scunthorpe
Provides basis for selecting NC subject-specific vocabulary to use with spelling strategies. Primary/lower secondary.

Palmer, Sue (1990) — ***Mind Your Spelling*** — Oliver and Boyd Harlow, Essex
Series of four work books with colourful illustrations to outline spelling strategies, including rules. Primary.

Peters, Margaret L. and Smith, Brigid (1993) — ***Spelling in Context*** — NFER Nelson Windsor
Strategies for teachers and learners including diagnostic spelling in relation to the developmental stages of spelling.

Ramsden, Mervyn (1993) — ***Rescuing Spelling*** — Southgate Books Crediton, Devon
Applying spelling to think about the development of language. Using matrices as a key teaching tool in activities and worksheets. Primary.

Stirling, E. G. (1992) — ***Subject Spellchecks*** — 114 Westbourne Rd Sheffield, S10 2QT
List of keywords in specialist subjects for KS4 examinations. Very useful.

Topping, K.J. (1992) — ***Cued Spelling Training Tape*** — Kirklees Metropolitan Council
Same principles as paired reading. Highly interactive. Encourages 'self-managed' learning of spelling. Primary.

Webster, Alec and Webster, Valerie (1994) — ***Supporting Learning in the Primary School*** — Avec Designs Bristol
Spelling strategies and graded NC levels suitable for setting IEP literacy targets.

Wilson, Jo (1993) — ***P.A.T. Phonological Awareness Training*** — Education Publications University College London
Three booklets containing a new approach to phonics. Primary and secondary.